Steffen Kirilmaz

The meaning of Americanisation illustrated by the example of the global player "Abercrombie and Fitch"

GRIN Verlag

Bibliografische Information der Deutschen Nationalbibliothek:

Die Deutsche Bibliothek verzeichnet diese Publikation in der Deutschen National-
bibliografie; detaillierte bibliografische Daten sind im Internet über http://dnb.d-
nb.de/ abrufbar.

Impressum:

Copyright © 2011 GRIN Verlag, Open Publishing GmbH
Druck und Bindung: Books on Demand GmbH, Norderstedt Germany
ISBN: 978-3-640-87285-5

Dieses Buch bei GRIN:

http://www.grin.com/de/e-book/169155/the-meaning-of-americanisation-illustrated-
by-the-example-of-the-global

The meaning of Americanisation illustrated by the example of the global player "Abercrombie and Fitch"

Facharbeit
von

Steffen Kirilmaz

1. Leistungskurs Englisch
Jahrgangsstufe 12/II
Schuljahr 2010/11

Geschwister-Scholl-Gymnasium
Pulheim

Table of Contents

1 Introduction 3

2 Americanisation 3

      2.1 Definition 3
      2.2 Historical development 4
      2.3 Current situation 5

3 Abercrombie and Fitch 7

      3.1 Abercrombie a global player 7
      3.2 Abercrombie's secret of success 9

4 Abercrombie a part of Americanisation 12

5 Conclusion.. 13

6 References... 14

7 Appendix.. 15

1 Introduction

"The illusion of America as a wonderland will continue as long as...
...it's profitable to continue the illusion. At the point where the
illusion becomes too expensive to maintain, they will just take down
the scenery, they will move the tables and chairs out of the way,
then they will pull back the curtains and you will see the brick wall at
the back of the theatre." (Frank Zappa) [1]

Frank Zappa used this phrase to show the capitalistic policy in America
and its successful way in spreading out its mass culture all over the world.
What is it, that fascinates so much that one wants to live the "American
way/dream"? Wear the same things like Americans? BE like Americans?
That is the question that I am nterested in and which I want to solve in my
skilled work.

I have been to the USA a few times and I have seen myself going through
the process of being manipulated in a kind of way that convinced me of an
America as a place seemingly with no boundaries where everything
seems to be possible. Therefore I want to look behind the scenes of the
idealisation of this country and show how it has changed during the last
few decades. I will point out the development of Americanisation together
with the connected changes of culture and society that follow. I will use the
example of the global player and fashion brand Abercrombie and Fitch to
illustrate this development and I will clarify how this company makes use
of the position of America as a global role-model to successfully apply their
marketing strategies.

2 Americanisation
2.1 Definition of Americanisation

Americanisation describes the transfer of cultural objects from America to
other nations, and the connected changes in the areas of economy,
politics and culture that follow. Those cultural objects are integrated into an

---

1   Frank Zappa (1940-1993) was a famous musician

existing system and change society in terms of institutions, values, traditions, language, behaviours. Also symbols, icons and pictures are taken over and copied from the USA.

This procedure is a one-sided interaction, that means it only runs in one direction, namely from the USA in other parts of the world. Examples for this procedure caused by Americanisation could be behavioural changes in language (e.g. by using Anglicisms), fashion trends, imported sports like American Football or Baseball and most probably the most significant example in nutrition habits going along with the consumption of fast food like "Mc Donald's"[2] or famous brands like "Coca Cola".

2.2 Historical development of Americanisation

Does the gap between Germany and America have to be as big as an ocean as it occurs today? The history of cultural transfer shows that it doesn't:

Since the first World War America is one of the most powerful economic nation in the world, and stands in the central perspective of many other countries. America was in ruling power of Germany after the war, therefore it had a significant influence in the development of the new structured Germany. The consequence of this surrendered rebuilding was the dependence on mass media (quick expansion of radio and TV) and a new way of education and politics in the country – a direct Americanisation means transfer of liberal mindset from the USA to Germany.

In the mid 50[s] the youth of Germany quickly became clearly influenced by the products coming from the USA. Jeans, Rock'n Roll and Hollywood became part of their own life and there was a great change in the cultural interaction between the people during that time: Demonstrated carelessness showed by their way of clothing, the way of communication by the use of Anglicisms like i.e. "Hobby", "Job" or "Computer" and the music they were listening to were unnoticed but permanent and consistent changes of daily life caused by the American influence.

---

2   See picture number 3 in appendix

To refer back to the question I raised earlier, of how America really did manage it to build a popular culture and a process of Americanization that fascinates countries from all over the world? The answer seems to be obvious and simple:

America's culture had to be Americanised itself first.[3] The multi-racial society of America led to an media market that had to reach all kind of people in the country. The result was a form of mass consumption of the media that no other country could offer at that time. It led to a production of simplification and reduction so that all kind of layers of the population were able to have access to cultural objects. So in other words the beginning of Americanisation can be retraced to the time when America started to simplify its culture to find the least common denominator of its population. [4]

In the last 10 years the term of Americanisation has been transformed into "Globalisation", which actually describes the transfer of cultural objects throughout the whole world,

> "[...] frequently it just seems to be another word for worldwide American influence" [5]

2.3 Current situation of Americanisation

Why does Germany's youth turn their baseball caps? Why do they break dance in the style of "the black Bloods of Los Angeles" to express their identity? Why is the American casual lifestyle so addictive? And why does the American culture displace the European one so quickly?

The most significant outcomes of Americanisation in society can be observed in the popular and everyday culture. Music, Film, TV and clothing are strongly influenced by the basic character of American culture. The mass media is the reason for the quick transfer of the American lifestyle to us, the rest of the world. The movie export from the US leaves the German studios no space for own productions, meaning we as a

---

3   cf. „Amerikanisierung – Globalisierung" by Winfried Fluck P.17, 11 f.
4   cf. „Amerikanisierung – Globalisierung" by Winfried Fluck P.17, 110 f.
5   „Americanization, Globalization, Education" (by Jürgen Donnerstag) P.69, 1.27 f.

society are seemingly watching only American sitcoms[6]. Therefore we actually live the American life through our television: We learn about their traditions and holidays like "Thanks Giving" and exports like "Halloween"; we admire their way of clothing, we get to know their actors, developing a virtual relationship which may cause them to become our role-models. Some of us even watch these movies in the original language just to see them the same way Americans do. The process of transferring ideas from the US can also strongly be observed in television shows like "Wer Wird Millionär" or "Deutschland sucht den Superstar". Those German TV shows are just copies of the American original idea.

The English language is another significant attribute that has lead to changes in our culture.

"The Global language opens the markets for American products [...]"[7]

and we get used to it so that we don't even notice English words anymore and integrate them in our lives like our native ones. The same thing happens in the music industry. Songs are getting imported and, further than that masses of teenagers identify themselves with those music stars living abroad . They observe their taste of fashion, their behaviour and language and copy it for their own way of living. In that age they are in a process of finding their identity and by copying American idols they are connected and dependent on the American way of life. It also seems to be important for teenagers to fit and to feel as though they belong to this society, and it may be these American idols, who help them to achieve this goal.

The position of America as a role-model has been idealised during the last decades. Although more and more people commute between America and Germany, although news is getting transferred between countries and all around the globe in a very short time, our image of America is still not advanced and detailed enough to be totally realistic. The distorted images that shaped our idea of the United States from the time when few people travelled back and forth have not disappeared, but have just been

6 See picture number 4 in appendix
7 „Americanization, Globalization, Education" (by Jürgen Donnerstag) P.69

modified by the better transportation network of today.[8] The phrase "American Dream" is still in the heads of many people around the world, who believe in America as a country where everything is possible just like the motto "From dishwasher to millionaire". The latest events, above all the bad crisis management of the USA during the economical crisis, led to many critical responses, which claim that America is slowly losing its position as a global role-model. The US-American nobel prize winner Paul Krugman thinks, that there will be a massive change for America, which will no longer be the pioneer in economy, politics and society :

> "Gone are the days, from Pax Britannica to Pax Americana, when Britain and the United States made the rules that others followed."[9]

It is obvious that new emerging global powers like China are preparing themselves to take over influence and strength from the US setting future trends and benchmarks in production, technology, ,-economically they already play a major role, but the adoption of their culture traits will chance and influence our tomorrow.

3 Abercrombie and Fitch

3.1 Abercrombie and Fitch – a global player

> "The company was originally established as Abercrombie Co. by David Abercrombie on June 4, 1892, in a small waterfront [...] in downtown Manhattan, New York" [10]

A regular customer of the shop, Ezra Fitch, was the co-producer of the company and joined it in 1904. The two owners however had different views of the future of the shop and went separate ways - Abercrombie sold his share in the company to Fitch in 1907. To that time Abercrombie and Fitch only sold outdoor goods to outdoorsmen[11], and was just a shdow of the successful company it was to become after Fitch's retirement.

In 1988 the company was sold to Mike Jeffries from Limited Brands, which

---

8   cf. „Mythos Amerikanisierung in Deutschland seit 1900" (by Frank Becker) p.9 l.27 f.
9   Paul Krugman is an Us-American professor for economics at the Princeton University
1 0   Wikipedia. "The History of Abercrombie and Fitch" (chapter "Foundation")
1 1   See picture number 2 in appendix

was already successful in popularising companies like "Victoria Secret". Jeffries brought a whole new teen image to A&F,

> "[...] as he realized that the retail market was rapidly growing at that time. He replaced the old conservative outdoorsmen fashion, which was only aiming at men, with "high-priced casual wear for both young men and women à la Ralph Lauren". [12]

Soon Abercrombie gained a great reputation in the fashion business and was soon to be one of the leading youth fashion brands on the market. The company produced an image of an own lifestyle and published its own catalogue/magazine, A&F Quarterly, featuring its clothing lines as well as articles on pop culture, sex, music, and other teen topics.

> "The changes initiated by Jeffries began paying off; sales increased from $85 million in 1992 to $165 million in 1994.[...] there were 67 A&F stores at the end of January 1995, compared to 49 a year earlier". [13]

In 2000 Abercrombie launched its latest lifestyle brand "Hollister" in Columbus, Ohio. It offers the same kind of style as its mother company and presents the theme of surfing and fun in the sun.

> "Ironically, few realized the new company was a part of the A&F empire and many considered Hollister a rival to A&F", [14]

which made this connection to another successful merchandising gag. However in 2005 Abercrombie's image took a serious hit: It was accused of racial discrimination by the U.S. Equal Employment Opportunity Commission. The company was being charged of having a too high percentage of white coloured staff in their shops and a unbalanced number of variety in their advertising catalogues. The company replied on the charges and paid 40 million dollars to Afro-American applicants and employees and promised a more even number of people with different ethnical backgrounds in the future.

---

1   2   http://www.referenceforbusiness.com/history2/98/Abercrombie-Fitch-Company.html

1   3   "Abercrombie and Fitch Company" by Company History (chapter: "Expansion and Independence: 1990s")

1 4   "Abercrombie and Fitch Company" by Company History (chapter: "Wider Horizons 2000")

Since the global economical crisis in 2008, the company has realised that it has to expand and export its shops from America to Asia and Europe. The main underlying causes were the bad sales and profit figures during the past 2 years. Ever since Abercrombie had been a company that was extraordinary to the Europeans, because of its exclusivity meaning being a brand, which was not possible to be purchased in their own countries and in general outside of the US. So many critics of the new strategy of global expansion take the view that Abercrombie loses its special flair by expanding their shops to other continents. The following years will show, if Abercrombie will be able to put those people to silence and prove that their decision was right.

3.2 Abercrombie's secret of success
(a special shopping experience)

When we are shopping, we look for something we like, something that suits us, something that we can identify ourselves with. But is it always just the product we buy or is there so much more sales strategy behind these pieces of fabric? The shopping experience has changed in the last few years and has transformed fashion companies like Abercrombie & Fitch, which uses its special image to sell their products and with them their own lifestyle. But how does this strategy work and why is it so successful?

Buying a product in an Abercrombie & Fitch store is more than just getting a new outfit. It is a step into a new world, a start into a new lifestyle. Market researcher Devon Brown rightly stated, "Abercrombie sells a cultural experience". It begins in front of the store via the stylish shop fronts: While most stores load every available space with posters and placards shouting out about reduced prices, Abercrombie stays with its strategies of overprints and pictures of physically attractive young models, who are the examples of ambition and something to aspire to for the customer. These perceptions on fashion are well thought-out and give you the feeling that you could be a part of this and belong to these people by simply just buying the products inside of the A&F store. It pretends to give a different sense of your own ideal self, another view of what one would like to be. Abercrombie uses these strategies to attract and retain their customers.

As you enter the shop you get the first impression of what is waiting for you inside. A model is already in position to take photos with you in the first part of the shop. He is topless, which could perhaps be seen as ironic for being an ambassador of a clothes store.[15] The same thing can be seen on the Abercrombie advertising bags, where the models are posing without clothes. The fact that people also use these bags at school, show that many teenagers aspire to this lifestyle brand and want to show to others that they are a part of its fashion.

After you have walked through the doors, and seen the model you arrive in the part of the shop which gives a whole new perception of a fashion store. While other companies would concentrate on presenting their products in a more simple way, Abercrombie's store gives you the feeling of being in a club or a disco.[16] The loud music gives the store a special, young vibe, "the air is full of the company's signature perfume and the whole environment seems to be dark yet exhilarating" [17]. The stores are also staffed with attractive "brand representatives", young sales people who show the Abercrombie & Fitch lifestyle: attractive, popular, enthusiastic, and outgoing. All these people have been carefully hand-picked for their jobs by the lure of being in-store models, rather than sales assistants to represent the cultural experience. Goffman[18] would point out the staff's way of styling because they wear the clothes of Abercrombie and Fitch, to again be a role model for the customer and not only sell, but live the lifestyle Abercrombie leads to. In fact all these factors you find in the store make you feel like a "hero" and you live this dream while you are in this artificial environment which is completely different of that of normal shopping stores. All these things distract you from the actual products Abercrombie sells and you just buy them to become a part of it.

The most significant of the company's lifestyle branding efforts was them producing an in-store magazine called Quarterly, which was highly

---

1 5 5   See picture number 1 in appendix
1 6   cf. Brand Communication at its best. (by Elemental Design)
1 7   cf. Brand Communication at its best. (by Elemental Design)
1 8   Erving Goffman was a canadian sociologist and writer

criticised by society, because of its special tactic of marketing. One single outlay for example featured more than one hundred pages of photographs depicting young-looking models posed in various stages of undress - In fact Abercrombie & Fitch follows straight the motto "sex sells"! But Abercrombie pulled the *Quarterly* from the store shelves after a few years. It is no longer available for purchase. While some sources have claimed this as a victory for the protesters, Abercrombie & Fitch denies that consumer complaints had anything to do with the magazine's removal. This might be a move to protect the image and kind of lifestyle of the company, because it shows that Abercrombie still stands behind its way of selling and presenting their products.

But what makes these products so attractive to people that motivates them to pay a fortune; even though the products obviously have just an average quality? Overall I think the reasons for that is the special way Abercrombie and Fitch presents and sells its products as elaborated before: Firstly the very unusual stores, which hold the customers tight from the first moment on and makes it unique to any other[19] – which aim to please and attract its customer, It doesn't just sell clothes, but it sells an image that appeals to a large audience, and connotes the idea of success and something for many people to aspire to. And Secondly the very magnificent image and lifestyle the company sells. I think that Abercrombie and Fitch has managed to reach a very powerful position on the fashion market. It can be recognised just about anywhere, not because of its style of clothes as such, but because of the ideas behind it.. The success of Abercrombie as company is remarkable: A years ago I have seen the hype of teenagers towards this company with my own eyes during my exchange year in England. There is nothing else to talk about in schools, but about the new collection and new sales staff in the stores of A&F. Its rebranding strategies, that made it a noble trendy brand was the best thing that could happen to this company.

---

1 9   See picture number 5 in appendix

4 Abercrombie - a part of Americanisation

When teenager turn into a certain age their appearance becomes more important for them. They are more interested in fashion, and clothing becomes something more than just items to protect them from the weather and cover them in a practical way, but more of an example of their identity and what they stand for. They are getting socialized into wanting to appear attractive to the opposite sex, and wanting to have a clear individual identity. Therefore clothing is an important attribute in teenagers lives and it is used by Abercrombie to connect them with the American world and the proposed and illustrated colourful own companies lifestyle. When teenager enter one of those shops they automatically dive into a prototype of the American culture. The customer is breathing American air like he was staying in an invisible bubble.

Entering the store means getting touched by several American influences which could be understood as different effects of Americanisation. Young people who are interested in buying A&F-Product experience the bonding between their new clothes and music: In the stores the songs of well known famous American charts players are presented. Music itself purchases our emotions. In this case the popular RnB, RAP, HipHop and Rock Music from overseas transports the US-atmosphere into the stores and combine it with the new fashion collection. The customer also realises the tie between clothes and attraction: as well as American actors and role models impose the German youth so does Abercrombie & Fitch sales assistants. They themselves are good looking and they represent American`s ideology of beauty.

The connection between A&F-clothes and American culture is further reinforced by the English language which is the main communication form. The advertising and whole promotion in and outside the stores is in English. Original price tags which are adapted later are still sticking on the clothing. Shopping in the store leads you to adapt yourself to the environment and might even make you switch your language and start speaking English.

The A&F stores on one hand and at least their fashion on the other hand work as a pipeline of American lifestyle. They transport many different facets of their culture which are welcomed in Europe. Teenagers from all over the world, who may decide to visit the USA, can visit one of Abercrombie's shops to get a souvenir of the American world in order to stay connected with it "the American Dream" even being back at home.

In summary it can be said that companies like Abercrombie lead to a consumption of American products and with it to an intake of the American life.

5 Conclusion

Are the young people, who are influenced by the American way of life, losing their identity and their freedom by imitating and taking over foreign products?

"A person, who is prepared to surrender his freedom to win security, will lose both". (Benjamin Franklin)[20]

When you put that quote in the context of Americanisation it might mean, that other countries make themselves dependent on America and lose their freedom and individuality, because of their habit in only copying the lives of others in order to gain the feeling of belonging to something that occurs meaningful to them. They proclaim to keep their identity although they put no effort in keeping their own culture free from being mixed up by America's. By just choosing to use some parts of this influence they believe to enrich their lives. This process leads to an Americanisation of the world and it limits and tightens the space for a variety of cultures and ways of living the individual way and quality of life.

We should keep the request, that the critical attitude towards American way of making politics, economies and environmental decisions will stay alive and keep unbroken. Herbert Grönemeyer shows a similar point of

2   0   Was one of the founding fathers of the United States of America

- 14 -

view in his song Amerika by saying: *"Du kommst als Retter in jeder Not zeigst der Welt deinen Sheriff Stern [...]Du hast viel für uns getan ... Tu uns das nicht an [...] Ich habe Angst vor deiner Phantasie vor deinem Ehrgeiz"[21]* he points out his own sceptical view: We should keep a healthy distance between us and the mighty and strong power, which could help and damage our country at the same time. However the Globalisation of the world can also have positive sides, but it is important that the singularity of different cultures is ensured. Companies like the just describes example of Abercrombie and Fitch present and simulate a way of life to its customers and offers therefore just an artificial world in its shops that surrenders the teenager and convinces them of an America as a country to admire and puts it that makes it seem to be a "wonderland".

6 References

Books:

Ute Bechdolf; Reinhard Johler; Horst Tonn. *Amerikanisierung Globalisierung – Transnationale Prozesse im europäischen Alltag.* Trier: wvt Verlag, 2007

Frank Becker; Elke Reinhardt Becker. *Mythos USA: Amerikanisierung in Deutschland seit 1900.* Frankfurt: Campus Verlag, 2006

Gerhard Bach; Sabine Broeck; Ulf Schulenberg. *Americanization – Globalization – Education.* Heidelberg: Universitätsverlag, 2003

Harm G. Schröter. Winners and Losers. *Eine kurze Geschichte der Amerikanisierung. 2008*

Websites:

Elemental Design. *Brand Communication at its best. URL:* www.elemental.co.uk/newsletters/news_01_07/PDFS/brand.pdf

Jörg Nowick, TextilWirtschaft online. *Abercrombie & Fitch: Deutschland – Premiere in Düsseldorf. URL:* www.textilwirtschaft.de/news/topnews/pages/abercrombie-

2 1 Herbert Grönemeyer, „Amerika" 14. August 1984

Fitch- Deutschland-Premiere-in-Düsseldorf_66059.html

Deluxe Label, Lifestyle Magazine. *Abercrombie & Fitch bald bei Hollister in Deutschland erhältlich. URL: www.deluxe-label.de/abercrombie-fitch-bald-bei-hollister-in-deutschland-erhaeltlich-343/*

Wikipedia, the free encyclopedia. History of Abercrombie and Fitch,URLhttp://en.wikipedia.org/wiki/History_of_Abercrombie _%26_Fitch

Yavi Bartula, Style ranking. News: Abercrombie and Fitch Store 2011 in Düsseldorf. URL: www.styleranking.de/news/fashion-news/abercrombie-fitch-store-bald-in-dusseldorf

Wikipedia, the free encyclopedia. *Amerikanisierung. URL:* http://de.wikipedia.org/wiki/Amerikanisierung

Company History Index, *Abercrombie and Fitch Company. URL:* http://www.referenceforbusiness.com/history2/98/Abercrombi e-Fitch-Company.html

Musik:

Herbert Grönemeyer, *Amerika, URL: www.youtube.com/watch? v=0lDop4kzFjl*

7 Appendix

Picture 1

An example of an Abercrombie and Fitch model, taking photos with a customer in front of one of the company's stores.

Source: Google
URL: ttp://2.bp.blogspot.com/_A-KzGO_salE/TGK8fLexl0I/AAAAAAAA
DBk/G6jB39eH6fk/s1600/P1040567.J
PG

Picture 2

Cover of the A&F catalog from 1909.

Source: Wikipedia   URL:
http://en.wikipedia.org/wiki/History_of_
Abercrombie_%26_Fitch

Picture 3

A picture of a fast food branch in Peking

Source: Spiegel
online   URL:
http://www.spiegel.
de/kultur/gesellscha
ft/0,1518,541420,0
0.html

Picture 4

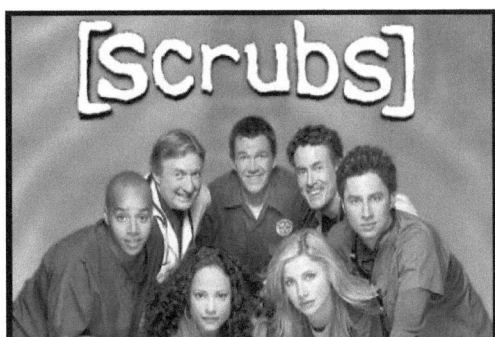

Scrubs, an example for an imported Sitcom from the US to Germany.

Source: Google
URL:
http://www.testedich.de/quiz23/picture/pic_118 6611850_1.jpg

Picture 5

A view inside of an typical A&F store: Special light effects are used to demonstrate very special atmosphere.

Source: Google
URL:
http://www.abercrombie.com/anf/careers/images/I-storeOpp_photo.jpg